HOW DO I KNOW GOD'S PURPOSE FOR MY LIFE?

JOHN RAGSDALE

SMITH
FREEMAN
Publishing

How Do I Know God's Purpose for My Life?

Bible verses were taken from the following translations:

Scripture quotations marked KJV are taken from The Holy Bible, King James Version. Public domain.

Scripture quotations marked HCSB are taken from the Holman Christian Standard Bible®, Copyright © 1999, 2000, 2002, 2003, 2009 by Holman Bible Publishers, Nashville, Tennessee. Used by permission. Holman Christian Standard Bible®, Holman CSB®, and Hcsb® are federally registered trademarks of Holman Bible Publishers.

Scripture quotations marked NASB are taken from the New American Standard Bible®, Copyright © 1960, 1962, 1963, 1968, 1971, 1972, 1973, 1975, 1977, 1995 by The Lockman Foundation. Used by permission. (www.Lockman.org)

Scripture quotations marked NCV are taken from the New Century Version. Copyright © 1987, 1988, 1991 by Thomas Nelson, Inc. Used by permission. All rights reserved.

Scripture quotations marked NIV are taken from The Holy Bible, New International Version®, NIV®. Copyright ©1973, 1978, 1984, 2011 by Biblica, Inc.™ Used by permission of Zondervan. All rights reserved worldwide. www.zondervan.com. The "NIV" and "New International Version" are trademarks registered in the United States Patent Office by Biblica, Inc.™

Scripture quotations marked NKJV are taken from the New King James Version®. Copyright © 1982 by Thomas Nelson. Used by permission. All rights reserved.

Scripture quotations marked NLT are taken from the Holy Bible, New Living Translation, copyright © 1996, 2004, 2015 by Tyndale House Foundation. Used by permission of Tyndale House Publishers, Inc., Carol Stream, Illinois 60188. All rights reserved.

ISBN: 978-0-9986529-5-5

ABOUT THE AUTHOR

John Ragsdale is a husband (to Kristin), a daddy (to Evan and Davis), a lover of Jesus, a singer-songwriter, a passionate communicator, and pastor of The Hills Nashville.

CONTENTS

A Message to Readers.. 5

Seven Steps to Help You Discover
God's Purpose for Your Life 7

1. Discovering Your Purpose 8

2. Jesus: The Ultimate Example 14

3. God Has a Plan for You 20

4. Put God First.. 26

5. Pray about It... 32

6. Listen to God and Keep an Open Mind 38

7. Consider the Disciples: We All Have
   the Same Commission 44

8. Keep Searching for Wisdom 50

9. Start Where You Are: Home,
   Work, Church, Community 56

10. Get Going 62

11. Focus... 68

12. Your Daily Planning Session 74

13. Believe 80

14. Mid-Course Corrections............................... 86

15. Rediscovering Your Purpose
    When Times Are Tough................................ 92

16. Trust and Obey.. 98

17. You Don't Have to Do It Alone 104

18. Trust His Timing.. 110

19. You Are a Disciple 116

20. Perspective and Peace................................. 122

A MESSAGE TO READERS

What does God want me to do with my life? That's a question that you may have asked yourself on many occasions. Although your vision of God's plan may be clouded or vague, you can be sure that the Lord's vision is crystal clear. He has a plan for everything, including you. As a part of that plan, He intends that you experience peace and spiritual abundance here on earth and eternal life with Him in heaven.

The ideas on these pages are intended as tools to assist you in discovering the unfolding plans and purposes that God has in store for you. This text does not attempt to answer every question concerning your particular situation. Instead, it gives you time-tested, biblically based directions for the journey ahead.

If you sincerely seek God's guidance for your life, He will give it. But He will make His revelations known to you in a way and in a time of His choosing, not yours. So if you're sincerely seeking to know God's will for your life, don't be worried if you haven't yet received a "final" answer. The final answer, of course, will come not in this world, but in the next.

With God as your shepherd, you have nothing to fear. So instead of fretting about the future, open your heart to Him in the present moment. Listen to Him, and do the work that He has placed before you. Then rest assured that if you genuinely trust God and accept the salvation of His only begotten Son, God's plans for you will be as perfect as His love.

SEVEN STEPS TO HELP YOU DISCOVER GOD'S PURPOSE FOR YOUR LIFE

Remember that God already has a plan for you. God doesn't do things by accident. He created you for a particular purpose, and He has wonderful things in store for you.

Be receptive. God is constantly leading you in a direction of His choosing, but He's given you free will, the ability to make choices on your own. So it's up to you to be receptive to His guidance. How? You can start with lots of prayer, regular worship, consistent Bible study, and a regular daily devotional.

Be obedient. You're more likely to sense His guidance—and hear His voice— when you're walking in the light.

Be patient. God's timing is best, so don't be discouraged if things don't work out as quickly as you wish. Instead of worrying about your future, entrust it to God.

Be a disciple. Ultimately, your purpose will be defined by your relationship with Jesus. We are all called to follow in Christ's footsteps. You owe it to yourself, to your family, and to your Creator to be a devoted disciple of the One from Galilee.

Ask and keep asking. When you ask for His guidance, prayerfully and often, He will respond in His own time and in His own way.

Get going. Usually it takes courage to answer God's call, especially if a big change is called for. But if you genuinely believe you're fulfilling God's purpose, the time to begin is now.

1

THE QUESTION

Sometimes I feel stuck,
and sometimes I feel confused.
How can I discover God's purpose for my life?

THE ANSWER

God's plans for you are unfolding day by day.
If you keep your eyes and your heart open,
He'll reveal those plans. God has big things
in store for you, but He may have quite a few
lessons to teach you before you are fully
prepared to do His will and fulfill His purposes.

*You will show me the path of life;
in Your presence is fullness of joy;
at Your right hand are pleasures forevermore.*

PSALM 16:11 NKJV

DISCOVERING YOUR PURPOSE

*We have also received an inheritance in Him,
predestined according to the purpose
of the One who works out everything
in agreement with the decision of His will.*

EPHESIANS 1:11 HCSB

God doesn't do things by accident. He didn't put you here by chance. The Lord didn't deliver you to your particular place, at this particular time, with your particular set of talents and opportunities on a whim. He has a plan, a one-of-a-kind mission designed especially for you. Discovering that plan may take time. But if you keep asking God for guidance, He'll lead you along a path of His choosing and give you every tool you need to fulfill His will.

Of course, you'll probably encounter a few impediments as you attempt to discover the exact nature of God's purpose for your life. And you may travel down a few dead ends along the way. But if you keep searching, and if you genuinely seek the Lord's guidance, He'll reveal His plans at a time and place of His own choosing.

Today and every day, God is beckoning you to hear His voice and follow His plan for your life. When you listen—and when you answer His call—you'll be amazed at the wonderful things an all-knowing, all-powerful God can do.

MORE FROM GOD'S WORD

*We must do the works of Him who sent Me while
it is day. Night is coming when no one can work.*
JOHN 9:4 HCSB

*And whatever you do, do it heartily,
as to the Lord and not to men.*
COLOSSIANS 3:23 NKJV

*For we are His creation, created in Christ Jesus
for good works, which God prepared ahead
of time so that we should walk in them.*
EPHESIANS 2:10 HCSB

*For we are God's coworkers.
You are God's field, God's building.*
1 CORINTHIANS 3:9 HCSB

*So whether you eat or drink, or whatever you do,
do it all for the glory of God.*
1 CORINTHIANS 10:31 NLT

MORE THOUGHTS
ABOUT PURPOSE

*There's some task which the God of all the universe,
the great Creator, has for you to do, and which will
remain undone and incomplete, until by faith
and obedience, you step into the will of God.*

ALAN REDPATH

*You weren't an accident. You weren't mass
produced. You aren't an assembly-line product.
You were deliberately planned,
specifically gifted, and lovingly positioned
on the Earth by the Master Craftsman.*

MAX LUCADO

Live out your life in its full meaning; it is God's life.

JOSIAH ROYCE

*All of God's people are ordinary people
who have been made extraordinary
by the purpose He has given them.*

OSWALD CHAMBERS

*The easiest way to discover the purpose of an
invention is to ask the creator of it. The same is true
for discovering your life's purpose: Ask God.*

RICK WARREN

REMEMBER THIS

God has big things in store for you, but He may have quite a few lessons to teach you before you are fully prepared to fulfill His purposes. So be patient, be watchful, keep working, and keep praying. Divine help is on the way.

GET PRACTICAL

Grab a sheet of paper and jot down a brief personal mission statement. But don't stop there. Keep refining your mission statement until you're confident that it reflects your talents, your opportunities, your passion, and God's will for your life.

—⁓—

A CONVERSATION STARTER

Talk to a friend about specific ways you can hear God's voice and follow His path.

NOTES TO YOURSELF

THOUGHTS ABOUT GOD'S DIRECTION

Write down a few things you feel God may be calling you to do this year. Have you answered the call yet?

....

....

....

....

....

....

....

....

....

....

2

THE QUESTION

What does Jesus have to do with my personal search for purpose and meaning?

THE ANSWER

God's Word promises that Jesus is the light of the world. And the Lord wants His Son to be the light of your life. Your intentions should be the same.

The deeper Christian life is the willingness to quit trying to use the Lord for our ends and let Him work in us for His glory.

A. W. TOZER

JESUS:
THE ULTIMATE EXAMPLE

Jesus Christ the same yesterday,
and today, and for ever.

HEBREWS 13:8 KJV

Jesus is the ultimate example of someone who fulfilled His purpose. He did it by focusing on one thing: He was determined to fulfill the will of God. Jesus said, "For I have come down from heaven to do the will of God who sent me, not to do my own will" (John 6:38 NLT).

Jesus never had to ask Himself His purpose because He knew His purpose was to fulfill the Father's plan. This helped Him make the right decision in His toughest time: "Father, if you are willing, take this cup from me; yet not my will, but yours be done" (Luke 22:42 NIV).

God had a plan for Jesus, and He has a plan for you. When you fulfill God's plan you will find and fulfill your purpose for living. The Lord intends to use you in wonderful, unexpected ways if you let Him, but be forewarned: the decision to seek God's plan and fulfill His purpose is yours and yours alone. The consequences of that decision have implications that are both profound and eternal, so choose carefully. And as you go about your daily activities, keep your eyes and ears open, as well as your heart.

MORE FROM GOD'S WORD

Who can separate us from the love of Christ?
Can affliction or anguish or persecution
or famine or nakedness or danger or sword?...
No, in all these things we are more than
victorious through Him who loved us.
ROMANS 8:35, 37 HCSB

The thief's purpose is to steal and kill and destroy.
My purpose is to give them a rich and satisfying life.
JOHN 10:10 NLT

I have come as a light into the world, that whoever
believes in Me should not abide in darkness.
JOHN 12:46 NKJV

I am the good shepherd. The good shepherd
gives His life for the sheep.
JOHN 10:11 NKJV

The next day John saw Jesus coming toward him
and said, "Here is the Lamb of God,
who takes away the sin of the world!"
JOHN 1:29 HCSB

MORE THOUGHTS
ABOUT JESUS

*We may blunder on for years thinking we know a
great deal about Him, and then, perhaps suddenly,
we catch a sight of Him as He is revealed in the
face of Jesus Christ, and we discover the real God.*

HANNAH WHITALL SMITH

*Ultimately, our relationship with Christ
is the one thing we cannot do without.*

BETH MOORE

*Jesus Christ is the first and last, author and finisher,
beginning and end, alpha and omega,
and by Him all other things hold together.
He must be first or nothing. God never comes next!*

VANCE HAVNER

*The crucial question for each of us is this:
What do you think of Jesus, and do you yet have
a personal acquaintance with Him?*

HANNAH WHITALL SMITH

*Trust God's Word and His power more than you trust
your own feelings and experiences. Remember,
your Rock is Christ, and it is the sea that ebbs
and flows with the tides, not Him.*

LETTIE COWMAN

REMEMBER THIS

An old hymn begins, "What a friend we have in Jesus." How true. Jesus is, indeed, the sovereign friend and ultimate Savior of mankind. May we all follow Him, praise Him, and share His message of salvation with our neighbors and with the world.

GET PRACTICAL

Jesus is the light of the world. Make sure that you are capturing and reflecting His light.

—*⁓*—

A CONVERSATION STARTER

Talk to a friend about what it means to be a true disciple of Jesus.

NOTES TO YOURSELF
YOUR RELATIONSHIP WITH JESUS

Write down your thoughts about Jesus: what He means to you and how your life has been changed by Him.

....

....

....

....

....

....

....

....

....

....

3

THE QUESTION

I want to understand God's plan for my life.
What does His Word say about that?

THE ANSWER

The Bible promises that God has a wonderful
plan for you. And the time to start looking for that
plan—and living it—is now. Discovering God's
plan begins with prayer, but it doesn't end there.
You've also got to work at it.

*God always gives His very best to those
who leave the choice with Him.*

Hudson Taylor

GOD HAS A PLAN FOR YOU

But as it is written: What eye did not see and ear did not hear, and what never entered the human mind—God prepared this for those who love Him.

1 CORINTHIANS 2:9 HCSB

God has a plan for this world and for your world. It's a plan that He understands perfectly, a plan that can bring you untold joy now and throughout eternity. But the Lord won't force His plan upon you. He's given you free will, the ability to make choices on your own. The totality of those choices will determine how well you fulfill God's calling.

Sometimes God makes Himself known in obvious ways, but more often His guidance is subtle. So we must be quiet to hear His voice.

If you're serious about discovering God's plan for your life—or rediscovering it—start spending quiet time with Him every day. Ask Him for direction. Pray for clarity. And be watchful for His signs. The more time you spend with Him, the sooner the answers will come.

MORE FROM GOD'S WORD

It is God who is at work in you, both to will and to work for His good pleasure.

PHILIPPIANS 2:13 NASB

We must do the works of Him who sent Me while it is day. Night is coming when no one can work.

JOHN 9:4 HCSB

For whoever does the will of God is My brother and My sister and mother.

MARK 3:35 NKJV

And yet, O LORD, you are our Father. We are the clay, and you are the potter. We are all formed by your hand.

ISAIAH 64:8 NLT

For My thoughts are not your thoughts, and your ways are not My ways.... For as heaven is higher than earth, so My ways are higher than your ways, and My thoughts than your thoughts.

ISAIAH 55:8–9 HCSB

MORE THOUGHTS
ABOUT GOD'S PLAN

*God's purpose is greater than our problems,
our pain, and even our sin.*

RICK WARREN

*If not a sparrow falls upon the ground without
your Father, you have reason to see that the
smallest events of your career are arranged by Him.*

C. H. SPURGEON

*Every experience God gives us, every person He
brings into our lives, is the perfect preparation for
the future that only He can see.*

CORRIE TEN BOOM

*God has a course mapped out for your life, and all
the inadequacies in the world will not change His
mind. He will be with you every step of the way.*

CHARLES STANLEY

*God has no problems, only plans.
There is never panic in heaven.*

CORRIE TEN BOOM

REMEMBER THIS

God has a plan for the world and for you. When you discover His plan for your life—and when you follow in the footsteps of His Son—you will be rewarded. The place where God is leading you is the place where you must go.

GET PRACTICAL

God has a wonderful plan for your life. And the time to start looking for that plan—and living it—is now. Discovering God's plan begins with prayer, but it doesn't end there. You've also got to work at it.

—⁕—

A CONVERSATION STARTER

Talk to a friend about the need to seek God's guidance in every aspect of your lives.

NOTES TO YOURSELF
THOUGHTS ABOUT GOD'S PLAN

Write down your thoughts about the importance of seeking God's guidance in every aspect of your life.

....

....

....

....

....

....

....

....

....

....

4

THE QUESTION

I have so many things to do and so many responsibilities to fulfill. So it's hard to make time for God. What does the Bible say about putting God first in my life?

THE ANSWER

God's Word is clear: If you put Him first in every aspect of your life, you'll be blessed. But if you relegate God to a position of lesser importance, you'll suffer the inevitable consequences that result from misplaced priorities.

We live in a hostile world that constantly seeks to pull us away from God.

BILLY GRAHAM

PUT GOD FIRST

You shall have no other gods before Me.
EXODUS 20:3 NKJV

For most of us, these are very busy times. We have obligations at home, at work, at school, or on social media. From the moment we rise until we drift off to sleep at night, we have things to do and people to contact. So how do we find time for God? We must make time for Him, plain and simple. When we put God first, we're blessed. But when we succumb to the pressures and temptations of the world, we inevitably pay a price for our misguided priorities.

In the book of Exodus, God warns that we should put no gods before Him. Yet all too often we place our Lord in second, third, or fourth place as we focus on other things. When we place our desires for possessions and status above our love for God—or when we yield to the countless distractions that surround us—we forfeit the peace that might otherwise be ours.

In the wilderness, Satan offered Jesus earthly power and unimaginable riches, but Jesus refused. Instead, He chose to worship His heavenly Father. We must do likewise by putting God first and worshiping Him only. God must come first. Always first.

MORE FROM GOD'S WORD

*Jesus said to him, " 'You shall love the Lord
your God with all your heart, with all your soul,
and with all your mind.' This is the first and
great commandment."*
MATTHEW 22:37–38 NKJV

Be careful not to forget the LORD.
DEUTERONOMY 6:12 HCSB

*No one can serve two masters. For you will
hate one and love the other; you will be devoted
to one and despise the other. You cannot serve
God and be enslaved to money.*
LUKE 16:13 NLT

*Do not love the world or the things that belong
to the world. If anyone loves the world,
love for the Father is not in him.*
1 JOHN 2:15 HCSB

*With my whole heart I have sought You;
Oh, let me not wander from Your commandments!*
PSALM 119:10 NKJV

MORE THOUGHTS
ABOUT PUTTING GOD FIRST

God wants to be in our leisure time as much as
He is in our churches and in our work.

BETH MOORE

Even the most routine part of your day can be
a spiritual act of worship.

SARAH YOUNG

Once we recognize our need for Jesus,
then the building of our faith begins. It is a daily,
moment-by-moment life of absolute
dependence upon Him for everything.

CATHERINE MARSHALL

Christ is either Lord of all, or He is not Lord at all.

HUDSON TAYLOR

The most important thing you must decide to do
every day is put the Lord first.

ELIZABETH GEORGE

REMEMBER THIS

God wants first place in your heart, and He wants you to follow in the footsteps of His Son. When you alter your life by putting God first, you will be blessed now and forever.

GET PRACTICAL

Think about specific ways that you can honor God by placing Him first in your life. God deserves first place in your heart, and you'll be blessed when you put Him there.

A CONVERSATION STARTER

Talk to a friend about what it means to put God first.

NOTES TO YOURSELF
PUTTING GOD FIRST

Write down your thoughts about the importance of putting God first and the dangers of putting the world's values
ahead of His commandments.

5

THE QUESTION

I know that I should probably pray more about God's plan for my life, but it seems like I never quite get around to it. What does the Bible say about prayer?

THE ANSWER

God's Word teaches us that prayer is an essential part of a well-lived life. One way to make sure that your heart is in tune with God is to pray often. The more you talk to Him, the more He will talk to you.

And if you believe, you will receive whatever you ask for in prayer.

Matthew 21:22 HCSB

PRAY ABOUT IT

Rejoice always, pray without ceasing,
in everything give thanks; for this is the will of God
in Christ Jesus for you.
1 Thessalonians 5:16–18 NKJV

Perhaps, on occasion, you may find yourself overwhelmed by the press of everyday life. Perhaps you may forget to slow yourself down long enough to talk with God. Instead of turning your thoughts and prayers to Him, you may rely upon your own resources. Instead of asking God for guidance, you may depend only upon your own limited wisdom. A far better course of action is this: Simply stop what you're doing long enough to open your heart to God; then listen carefully for His directions. In all things great and small, seek God's wisdom and His grace. He hears your prayers, and He will answer. All you must do is ask.

Prayer is a powerful tool that you can use to change your world and change yourself. God hears every prayer and responds in His own way and according to His own timetable. When you make a habit of consulting Him about everything, He'll guide you along a path of His choosing, which, by the way, is the path you should take. And when you petition Him for strength, He'll give you the courage to face any problem and the power to meet any challenge. So today, instead of turning things over in your mind, turn them over to God in prayer. Take your concerns to the Lord and leave them there. Your heavenly Father is listening, and He wants to hear from you. Now.

MORE FROM GOD'S WORD

*And whenever you stand praying, if you
have anything against anyone, forgive him,
so that your Father in heaven may also
forgive you your wrongdoing.*

Mark 11:25 HCSB

*Ask, and it will be given to you; seek, and you
will find; knock, and it will be opened to you. For
everyone who asks receives, and he who seeks
finds, and to him who knocks it will be opened.*

Matthew 7:7–8 NASB

*Confess your trespasses to one another,
and pray for one another, that you
may be healed. The effective, fervent prayer
of a righteous man avails much.*

James 5:16 NKJV

Is anyone among you suffering? He should pray.

James 5:13 HCSB

*I desire therefore that the men pray everywhere,
lifting up holy hands, without wrath and doubting.*

1 Timothy 2:8 NKJV

MORE THOUGHTS ABOUT PRAYER

Don't pray when you feel like it. Have an appointment with the Lord and keep it.

CORRIE TEN BOOM

Two wings are necessary to lift our souls toward God: prayer and praise. Prayer asks. Praise accepts the answer.

LETTIE COWMAN

Any concern that is too small to be turned into a prayer is too small to be made into a burden.

CORRIE TEN BOOM

It is impossible to overstate the need for prayer in the fabric of family life.

JAMES DOBSON

Prayer is our lifeline to God.

BILLY GRAHAM

REMEMBER THIS

If you're having troubles of any sort, pray about them. Prayer changes things, and it changes you. So pray.

GET PRACTICAL

If you can't seem to hear God, go to a quiet place and ask for His help. If you ask, and keep asking, He'll heal your heart and guide your path.

—⁓—

A CONVERSATION STARTER

Talk to a friend about your experiences concerning prayer: times when your prayer life was meaningful and times when you found it hard to pray. How did the quality and quantity of your prayers impact the other aspects of your life?

NOTES TO YOURSELF
THE POWER OF PRAYER

Write down your thoughts about the power of prayer.

....

....

....

....

....

....

....

....

....

....

6

THE QUESTION

I can talk to God, but I have trouble waiting
for His answers. What does the Bible say
about listening to God?

THE ANSWER

Whether you are communicating with God or with
other people, its always a good idea
to listen more than you talk.

*The purpose of all prayer is to find God's will
and to make that our prayer.*

CATHERINE MARSHALL

LISTEN TO GOD AND KEEP AN OPEN MIND

Be still, and know that I am God.
PSALM 46:10 KJV

As you search for purpose and meaning in your life, be sure to talk often with your heavenly Father. And after you've finished talking, be sure to listen carefully for His reply.

God speaks to us in different ways at different times. Sometimes He speaks loudly and clearly. But more often, He speaks in a quiet voice that's best heard in silence. So you must carve out quiet moments each day to study His Word and to sense His direction.

Are you willing to pray sincerely and then to wait quietly for God's response? Can you quiet yourself long enough to listen to your conscience? Are you attuned to the subtle guidance of your intuition? Hopefully so. Usually God refrains from sending His messages on stone tablets or city billboards. More often, He communicates in subtler ways. If you sincerely desire to hear His voice, you must listen carefully, and you must do so in the silent corners of your quiet, willing heart.

MORE FROM GOD'S WORD

The one who is from God listens to God's words.
This is why you don't listen, because you
are not from God.
JOHN 8:47 HCSB

Be silent before Me.
ISAIAH 41:1 HCSB

Listen, listen to me, and eat what is good,
and you will delight in the richest of fare.
Give ear and come to me; listen, that you may live.
ISAIAH 55:2–3 NIV

Rest in the LORD, and wait patiently for Him.
PSALM 37:7 NKJV

In quietness and in confidence
shall be your strength.
ISAIAH 30:15 KJV

MORE THOUGHTS
ABOUT LISTENING TO GOD

*Prayer is not monologue, but dialogue. God's voice
in response to mine is its most essential part.*

ANDREW MURRAY

*Deep within the center of the soul is a
chamber of peace where God lives and where,
if we will enter it and quiet all the other sounds,
we can hear His gentle whisper.*

LETTIE COWMAN

*If you, too, will learn to wait upon God, to get
alone with Him, and remain silent so that you can
hear His voice when He is ready to speak to you,
what a difference it will make in your life!*

KAY ARTHUR

*God's voice is still and quiet and easily buried
under an avalanche of clamor.*

CHARLES STANLEY

*When God speaks to us,
He should have our full attention.*

BILLY GRAHAM

REMEMBER THIS

Prayer is two-way communication with God. Talking to God isn't enough; you should also listen to Him. He has many things He wants to tell you. The better you listen, the more you'll learn.

GET PRACTICAL

If you want to have a meaningful conversation with God, don't make Him shout. Instead, go to a quiet place and listen. If you keep listening long enough and carefully enough, the Lord will talk directly to you.

―∿―

A CONVERSATION STARTER

Talk to a friend about the ways that God speaks to His believers.

NOTES TO YOURSELF
LISTENING CAREFULLY FOR GOD'S VOICE

Write down your thoughts about the importance of listening to God and the need to follow His calling.

....

....

....

....

....

....

....

....

....

....

....

....

....

....

....

....

....

7

THE QUESTION

I want to sense a calling from God.
What does the Bible say about that?

THE ANSWER

God knows you better than you know yourself.
He calls you to a life that is perfectly designed for
you, a life that will bring meaning, satisfaction,
and joy to yourself and to others.

—⁓—

*There's some task which the God of all the universe,
the great Creator, has for you to do, and which
will remain undone and incomplete, until by faith
and obedience, you step into the will of God.*

ALAN REDPATH

CONSIDER THE DISCIPLES: WE ALL HAVE THE SAME COMMISSION

I urge you to live a life worthy of the calling you have received.

EPHESIANS 4:1 NIV

God created you on purpose. He has a plan for your life that only you, with your unique array of talents and your own particular set of circumstances, can fulfill. The Lord is calling you; He's gently guiding you to the place where you can accomplish the greatest good for yourself and for His kingdom.

Have you already heard God's call? And are you doing your best to pursue His plan for your life? If so, you're blessed. But if you have not yet discovered God's plan for your life, don't panic. There's still time to hear His call and to follow His path. To find that path, keep searching and keep praying. Answers will come.

The Creator has placed you in a particular location, amid particular people, with unique opportunities to serve. And He has given you all the tools you need to accomplish His plans. So listen for His voice, watch for His signs, and prepare yourself for the call—His call—that is certain to come.

MORE FROM GOD'S WORD

For many are called, but few are chosen.
MATTHEW 22:14 KJV

For you have need of endurance, so that
when you have done the will of God,
you may receive the promise.
HEBREWS 10:36 NASB

For whoever does the will of God is
My brother and My sister and mother.
MARK 3:35 NKJV

And we know that all things work together for
good to those who love God, to those who
are the called according to His purpose.
ROMANS 8:28 NKJV

But as God has distributed to each one,
as the Lord has called each one, so let him walk.
1 CORINTHIANS 7:17 NKJV

MORE THOUGHTS
ABOUT GOD'S CALLING

*Whether you have twenty years left, ten years, one
year, one month, one day, or just one hour, there
is something very important God wants you to do
that can add to His kingdom and your blessing.*

BILL BRIGHT

*God's call is an inner conviction given
by the Holy Spirit and confirmed by the Word
of God and the body of Christ.*

ERWIN LUTZER

*It's important that you keep asking God to
show you what He wants you to do.
If you don't ask, you won't know.*

STORMIE OMARTIAN

*God never calls a person into His service
without equipping him.*

BILLY GRAHAM

*God will help us become the people we
are meant to be, if only we will ask Him.*

HANNAH WHITALL SMITH

REMEMBER THIS

God has a plan for your life, a divine calling that only you can fulfill. How you choose to respond to His calling will determine the direction you take and the contributions you make.

GET PRACTICAL

God calls you to a life that is perfectly suited for you, a life that honors Him and serves His purposes. Ask yourself if you've been actively answering His call or secretly resisting it.

A CONVERSATION STARTER

Talk to a friend about God's calling: what it means to answer His call and why we're tempted to resist it.

NOTES TO YOURSELF
ANSWERING GOD'S CALL

Write down your thoughts about what it means to answer God's call. What is He calling you to do today?

....

....

....

....

....

....

....

....

....

....

....

8

THE QUESTION

I have important decisions to make, and I want to choose wisely. How do I become a wiser, more thoughtful person?

THE ANSWER

If you own a Bible, you already have access to the most important kind of wisdom: God's wisdom. Your job is to read, to understand, and to apply His teachings to your life, starting now and ending never.

The Reference Point for the Christian is the Bible. All values, judgments, and attitudes must be gauged in relationship to this Reference Point.

Ruth Bell Graham

KEEP SEARCHING FOR WISDOM

Get wisdom—how much better it is than gold!
And get understanding—it is preferable to silver.
PROVERBS 16:16 HCSB

As you continue your lifelong search for purpose and meaning, you'll need wisdom and lots of it. Thankfully, all the wisdom that you'll ever need to live a meaningful life can be found in a single book: the Bible. God's Word guides us along a path that leads to abundance and eternal life. When we embrace Biblical teachings and follow God's Son, we're protected. But when we wander from His path, we inevitably suffer the consequences of our mistaken priorities.

In theory, all of us would prefer to be wise, but not all of us are willing to make the sacrifices that are required to gain real wisdom. To become wise, we must do more than spout platitudes, recite verses, or repeat aphorisms. We must not only speak wisely; we must live wisely. We must not only learn the lessons of the Christian life; we must live by them.

Today, as you think about the best way to live and the best way to lead, remember that God's wisdom can be found in a book that's already on your bookshelf: His Book. Read, heed, and live accordingly.

MORE FROM GOD'S WORD

*The fear of the L*ord *is the beginning of knowledge,*
but fools despise wisdom and instruction.
PROVERBS 1:7 NKJV

But the wisdom that is from above is first pure,
then peaceable, gentle, willing to yield,
full of mercy and good fruits, without partiality
and without hypocrisy.
JAMES 3:17 NKJV

He that walketh with wise men shall be wise:
but a companion of fools shall be destroyed.
PROVERBS 13:20 KJV

But if any of you lacks wisdom, let him ask of God,
who gives to all generously and without reproach,
and it will be given to him.
JAMES 1:5 NASB

Who among you is wise and understanding?
Let him show by his good behavior his deeds
in the gentleness of wisdom.
JAMES 3:13 NASB

MORE THOUGHTS
ABOUT WISDOM

Wisdom is the power to see and the inclination to choose the best and highest goal, together with the surest means of attaining it.

J. I. PACKER

True wisdom is marked by willingness to listen and a sense of knowing when to yield.

ELIZABETH GEORGE

Knowledge can be found in books or in school. Wisdom, on the other hand, starts with God... and ends there.

MARIE T. FREEMAN

To know the will of God is the highest of all wisdom.

BILLY GRAHAM

Wisdom is the right use of knowledge. To know is not to be wise. There is no fool so great as the knowing fool. But, to know how to use knowledge is to have wisdom.

C. H. SPURGEON

REMEMBER THIS

You still have lots to learn about yourself. Sometimes God allows us to endure difficult circumstances so that we might grow and mature as Christians.

GET PRACTICAL

Make it a point to study God's Word every day. When you do, you'll become a better person and a better Christian.

—◈—

A CONVERSATION STARTER

Talk to a friend about ways that you both have matured during the last few years. Have tough times taught you lessons you couldn't have learned any other way?

NOTES TO YOURSELF
ACQUIRING WISDOM AND LIVING WISELY

Write down your thoughts about the rewards of lifetime learning and the joys of living wisely.

....

....

....

....

....

....

....

....

....

....

9

THE QUESTION

I'm looking for a new beginning.
Where should I start?

THE ANSWER

Start in the very place where God
has put you, and start today. Study His Word,
seek His guidance, follow His Son, and trust Him
to lead you on a path of His choosing.

*Relying on God has to begin all over again
every day as if nothing had yet been done.*

C. S. Lewis

START WHERE YOU ARE: HOME, WORK, CHURCH, COMMUNITY

Do not remember the former things, nor consider the things of old. Behold, I will do a new thing.
ISAIAH 43:18–19 NKJV

Our heavenly Father has the power to make all things new. When we go to Him with sincere hearts and willing hands, He renews our spirits and redirects our steps.

Are you searching for a new path or a new purpose? Is so, the Lord is waiting patiently to give you a fresh start. He's prepared to help you change your thoughts, rearrange your priorities, reset your goals, and transform your life. But it doesn't stop there. He's also made a standing offer to forgive your sins, to forget your failings, and to protect you throughout all eternity. All you must do is ask.

Are you ready for a new beginning? If so, today is the perfect day to claim it by making God your partner in every endeavor. He can make all things new, including you.

MORE FROM GOD'S WORD

Then the One seated on the throne said,
"Look! I am making everything new."
REVELATION 21:5 HCSB

"For I know the plans I have for you"—this is
the LORD's declaration—"plans for your welfare,
not for disaster, to give you a future and a hope."
JEREMIAH 29:11 HCSB

There is one thing I always do. Forgetting the past
and straining toward what is ahead,
I keep trying to reach the goal and get
the prize for which God called me.
PHILIPPIANS 3:13–14 NCV

You are being renewed in the spirit of your minds;
you put on the new self, the one
created according to God's likeness in
righteousness and purity of the truth.
EPHESIANS 4:23–24 HCSB

Your old sinful self has died, and your new life
is kept with Christ in God.
COLOSSIANS 3:3 NCV

MORE THOUGHTS
ABOUT NEW BEGINNINGS

The best preparation for the future is the present
well seen to, and the last duty done.
GEORGE MACDONALD

Each day you must say to yourself,
"Today I am going to begin."
JEAN PIERRE DE CAUSSADE

What saves a man is to take a step.
Then another step.
C. S. LEWIS

Are you in earnest? Seize this very minute.
What you can do, or dream you can, begin it.
Boldness has genius, power, and magic in it.
JOHANN WOLFGANG VON GOETHE

God specializes in giving people a fresh start.
RICK WARREN

REMEMBER THIS

God specializes in giving His children fresh starts. And, He wants you to make the most of every opportunity He sends your way.

GET PRACTICAL

If you're graduating into a new phase of life, be sure to make God your partner. If you do, He'll guide your steps; He'll help carry your burdens; and He'll help you focus on the things that really matter.

— ɷ —

A CONVERSATION STARTER

Talk to a friend about some of the big changes you've been considering. What's been holding you back?

NOTES TO YOURSELF
A FRESH START

Write down your thoughts about new beginnings in your own life.

....

....

....

....

....

....

....

....

....

....

....

....

....

....

....

....

10

THE QUESTION

Sometimes I know the thing that needs to be done, but taking action is hard. What should I do?

THE ANSWER

The habit of procrastination is often rooted in the fear of failure, the fear of discomfort, or the fear of embarrassment. Your challenge is to confront these fears and defeat them. Now. Whether you feel like it or not.

Nine-tenths of the difficulties are overcome when our hearts are ready to do the Lord's will.

GEORGE MÜLLER

GET GOING

But prove yourselves doers of the word, and not merely hearers who delude themselves.

JAMES 1:22 NASB

When something needs to be done, the best time to do it is now, not later. But we're tempted to do otherwise. When the task at hand is difficult or unpleasant, we're tempted to procrastinate. But procrastination is the enemy of progress and a stumbling block on the path to success.

If we are to be responsible believers, we must realize that it is never enough simply to hear the instructions of God; we must also live by them. And it is never enough to wait idly by while others do God's work here on earth; we, too, must act. Doing God's work is a responsibility that each of us must bear, and when we do, our loving heavenly Father rewards our efforts with a bountiful harvest.

So, if you'd like to jumpstart your career or your life, ask God to give you the strength and the wisdom to do first things first, even if the first thing is hard. And while you're at it, use this time-tested formula for success: employ less talk and more action. Why? Because actions indeed speak louder than words—always have, always will. And a thousand good intentions pale in comparison to a single good deed.

MORE FROM GOD'S WORD

*When you make a vow to God, do not delay to
fulfill it. He has no pleasure in fools; fulfill your vow.*
ECCLESIASTES 5:4 NIV

*Well done, good and faithful servant; you were
faithful over a few things, I will make you ruler over
many things. Enter into the joy of your lord.*
MATTHEW 25:21 NKJV

*Whenever we have the opportunity, we should
do good to everyone—especially to those
in the family of faith.*
GALATIANS 6:10 NLT

*Therefore, with your minds ready for action,
be serious and set your hope completely
on the grace to be brought to you
at the revelation of Jesus Christ.*
1 PETER 1:13 HCSB

*For the kingdom of God is not
a matter of talk but of power.*
1 CORINTHIANS 4:20 HCSB

MORE THOUGHTS ABOUT ACTION

Pray as though everything depended on God.
Work as though everything depended on you.

St. Augustine

The one word in the spiritual vocabulary is now.

Oswald Chambers

Authentic faith cannot help but act.

Beth Moore

The great paralysis of our heart is unbelief.

Oswald Chambers

Do noble things, not dream them all day long;
and so make life, death, and that vast forever
one grand, sweet song.

Charles Kingsley

REMEMBER THIS

When important work needs to be done or important decisions need to be made, it's tempting to procrastinate. But God's Word teaches us to be "doers of the Word," which means taking action even when we might prefer to do nothing.

GET PRACTICAL

Have you been putting off an important decision? If so, remember that the best time to answer God's calling—and the appropriate time do His work—is now.

A CONVERSATION STARTER

Talk to a friend about any important tasks that you've been putting off.

NOTES TO YOURSELF
DO IT NOW

List a few important things you need to do but have been
putting off (and why you may have been procrastinating).

....

....

....

....

....

....

....

....

....

....

....

....

....

....

....

....

11

THE QUESTION

Sometimes I have trouble focusing
my thoughts and energies. What does
the Bible say about that?

THE ANSWER

The Lord wants you to focus your thoughts,
your energies, your emotions, and your prayers
on the things that really matter, and that means
putting God first and everything else next.

*The most important thing you must decide to
do every day is put the Lord first.*

ELIZABETH GEORGE

FOCUS

Let your eyes look forward;
fix your gaze straight ahead.
PROVERBS 4:25 HCSB

What is your focus today? Are you willing to focus your thoughts and energies on God's blessings and upon His plan for your life? Or will you turn your thoughts to other things? Before you answer that question, consider this: the Lord created you in His own image, and He wants you to experience joy and abundance. But He will not force His joy upon you; you must claim it for yourself.

This day—and every day hereafter—is a chance to celebrate the life that God has given you. It is also a chance to give thanks to the One who has offered you more blessings than you can possibly count. So today, as you seek God's purpose for your life, focus on His love for you. Ask Him for guidance and answer His call. With God as your partner, you'll have every reason to think optimistically about yourself and your world. And you can then share your optimism with others. They'll be better for it, and so will you. But not necessarily in that order.

MORE FROM GOD'S WORD

One thing I do, forgetting those things which are behind and reaching forward to those things which are ahead, I press toward the goal for the prize of the upward call of God in Christ Jesus.

PHILIPPIANS 3:13–14 NKJV

But seek first the kingdom of God and His righteousness, and all these things will be provided for you.

MATTHEW 6:33 HCSB

Patient endurance is what you need now, so that you will continue to do God's will. Then you will receive all that he has promised.

HEBREWS 10:36 NLT

Trust in the LORD with all your heart, and do not rely on your own understanding; think about Him in all your ways, and He will guide you on the right paths.

PROVERBS 3:5–6 HCSB

Let us lay aside every weight, and the sin which so easily ensnares us, and let us run with endurance the race that is set before us.

HEBREWS 12:1 NKJV

MORE THOUGHTS
ABOUT FOCUS

Energy and time are limited entities.
Therefore, we need to use them wisely,
focusing on what is truly important.

SARAH YOUNG

Give me a person who says, "This one thing I do,"
and not "These fifty things I dabble in."

D. L. MOODY

There is nothing quite as potent as a focused life,
one lived on purpose.

RICK WARREN

It is important to set goals because if you
do not have a plan, a goal, a direction, a purpose,
and a focus, you are not going to accomplish
anything for the glory of God.

BILL BRIGHT

Let's face it. None of us can do a thousand things
to the glory of God. And, in our own
vain attempt to do so, we stand the risk of
forfeiting a precious thing.

BETH MOORE

REMEMBER THIS

First focus on God...and then everything else will come into focus.

GET PRACTICAL

Ask yourself if you're truly focusing your thoughts and energies on matters that are pleasing to God and beneficial to your family. Then ask your Creator to help you focus on His love, His Son, and His plan for your life.

—⚏—

A CONVERSATION STARTER

Talk to a friend about the dangers of spreading yourself too thin and the advantages of focusing your energies on a few important priorities.

NOTES TO YOURSELF
FINDING FOCUS

Write down your thoughts about the need to focus on important tasks, not distractions.

....

....

....

....

....

....

....

....

....

....

....

....

....

....

....

....

....

12

THE QUESTION

I can't always find time to study
my Bible every day. What does the Bible
say about my daily devotional?

THE ANSWER

Your Creator wants you to get reacquainted
with His Word every day. Would you like a
foolproof formula for a better life? Here it is:
stay in close contact with God.

*Truly my soul silently waits for God;
from Him comes my salvation.*

PSALM 62:1 NKJV

YOUR DAILY PLANNING SESSION

Morning by morning he wakens me and opens my understanding to his will. The Sovereign LORD has spoken to me, and I have listened.

ISAIAH 50:4–5 NLT

Every new day is a gift from the Creator, a gift that allows each of us to say, "Thank You," by spending time with the Giver. When we begin the day with our Bibles open and our hearts attuned to God, we are inevitably blessed by the promises we find in His Word.

During the quiet moments we spend with the Lord, He guides us; He leads us; He touches our hearts. These are precious moments that contribute to our spiritual growth. We need our daily devotions.

Each day of your life has 1,440 minutes, and God deserves a few of them. And you deserve the experience of spending a few quiet minutes every morning with your Creator. So if you haven't already done so, establish the habit of spending time with God every day of the week. It's a habit that will change your day and revolutionize your life. When you give the Lord your undivided attention, everything changes, including you.

MORE FROM GOD'S WORD

*Early the next morning, while it was still dark,
Jesus woke and left the house. He went
to a lonely place, where he prayed.*
MARK 1:35 NCV

*But grow in the grace and knowledge of our Lord
and Savior Jesus Christ. To Him be the glory
both now and to the day of eternity.*
2 PETER 3:18 HCSB

*Thy word is a lamp unto my feet,
and a light unto my path.*
PSALM 119:105 KJV

*Heaven and earth will pass away,
but My words will never pass away.*
MATTHEW 24:35 HCSB

*It is good to give thanks to the LORD, and to
sing praises to Your name, O Most High.*
PSALM 92:1 NKJV

MORE THOUGHTS ABOUT YOUR DAILY DEVOTIONAL

Begin each day with God.
It will change your priorities.
ELIZABETH GEORGE

Relying on God has to begin all over again
every day as if nothing had yet been done.
C. S. LEWIS

Whatever is your best time in the day,
give that to communion with God.
HUDSON TAYLOR

Doesn't God deserve the best minutes of your day?
BILLY GRAHAM

Make it the first morning business of your life to
understand some part of the Bible clearly, and
make it your daily business to obey it.
JOHN RUSKIN

REMEMBER THIS

A regular time of quiet reflection, prayer, and Bible study will allow you to praise your Creator, to focus your thoughts, and to seek God's guidance on matters great and small. Don't miss this opportunity.

GET PRACTICAL

Make an appointment with God and keep it. Bible study and prayer should be at the top of your daily to-do list, not the bottom. No time is more valuable than the time you spend with your Creator.

—◁▥▷—

A CONVERSATION STARTER

Talk to a friend about the ways that daily Bible study can change your day and your life.

NOTES TO YOURSELF
YOUR DAILY DEVOTIONAL

Write down your thoughts about the importance of a regular, meaningful daily devotional.

....

....

....

....

....

....

....

....

....

13

THE QUESTION

Life is hard sometimes, so it's hard
for me to be optimistic. What does the Bible
say about optimism?

THE ANSWER

God's Word promises that if you've given
your heart to Jesus, your eternal future is secure.
So even when times are tough,
you can be joyful, hopeful, and optimistic.

All things work together for good. Fret not, nor fear!

LETTIE COWMAN

BELIEVE

The LORD is my light and my salvation—
whom should I fear? The LORD is the stronghold
of my life—of whom should I be afraid?
PSALM 27:1 HCSB

Are you a passionate Christian who expects God to do big things in your life and in the lives of those around you? If you're a thinking Christian, you have every reason to be confident about your future here on earth and your eternal future in heaven. As English clergyman William Ralph Inge observed, "No Christian should be a pessimist, for Christianity is a system of radical optimism." Inge's observation is true, of course, but sometimes you may find yourself caught up in the inevitable complications of everyday living. When you find yourself fretting about the inevitable ups and downs of life here on earth, it's time to slow down, collect yourself, refocus your thoughts, and count your blessings.

God has made promises to you, and He will most certainly keep every one of them. So, you have every reason to be an optimist and no legitimate reason to ever abandon hope.

Today, as you think about your purpose and contemplate your future, trust your hopes, not your fears. And while you're at it, take time to celebrate God's blessings. His gifts are too numerous to calculate and too glorious to imagine. But it never hurts to try.

MORE FROM GOD'S WORD

This hope we have as an anchor of the soul,
a hope both sure and steadfast.
HEBREWS 6:19 NASB

Let us hold on to the confession of our hope
without wavering, for He who promised is faithful.
HEBREWS 10:23 HCSB

"I say this because I know what I am planning
for you," says the LORD. "I have good plans for you,
not plans to hurt you. I will give you hope
and a good future."
JEREMIAH 29:11 NCV

But if we look forward to something we don't yet
have, we must wait patiently and confidently.
ROMANS 8:25 NLT

Make me to hear joy and gladness.
PSALM 51:8 KJV

MORE THOUGHTS
ABOUT OPTIMISM

*When you have vision it affects your attitude.
Your attitude is optimistic rather than pessimistic.*

CHARLES SWINDOLL

*Positive thinking will let you do everything
better than negative thinking will.*

ZIG ZIGLAR

*No more imperfect thoughts. No more sad
memories. No more ignorance. My redeemed
body will have a redeemed mind. Grant me a
foretaste of that perfect mind as You mirror
Your thoughts in me today.*

JONI EARECKSON TADA

*Two types of voices command your attention
today. Negative ones fill your mind with doubt,
bitterness, and fear. Positive ones purvey hope and
strength. Which one will you choose to heed?*

MAX LUCADO

*The remarkable thing is, we have a choice
every day regarding the attitude
we will embrace for that day.*

CHARLES SWINDOLL

REMEMBER THIS

As a follower of Christ, you have every reason to be optimistic about your future here on earth and your future in heaven. God is good, and your eternal future is secure. So why not be an optimist?

GET PRACTICAL

Be a realistic optimist. Your attitude toward the future will help create your future. So think realistically about yourself and your situation while making a conscious effort to focus on your hopes, not your fears.

—ɷ—

A CONVERSATION STARTER

Talk to a friend about the potential rewards of optimism and the potential dangers of pessimism.

NOTES TO YOURSELF
THE POWER OF OPTIMISM

Write down your thoughts about the power of optimism and the dangers of pessimism.

....

....

....

....

....

....

....

....

....

....

....

....

....

....

....

....

....

14

THE QUESTION

The world is changing faster and faster.
What should I do?

THE ANSWER

If a big change is called for, don't be afraid to
make it. Sometimes one big leap is better
than a thousand small steps.

*God, grant me the serenity to accept the things
I cannot change; courage to change the
things I can; and wisdom to know the difference.*

REINHOLD NIEBUHR

MID-COURSE CORRECTIONS

To every thing there is a season, and a time to every purpose under the heaven.

ECCLESIASTES 3:1 KJV

Here in the twenty-first century, everyday life has become an exercise in managing change. Our circumstances change; our relationships change; our bodies change. We grow older every day, as does our world. Thankfully, God does not change. He is eternal, as are the truths that are found in His holy Word.

On occasion, we all must endure life-altering losses that leave us breathless. When we do, our loving heavenly Father stands ready to protect us, to comfort us, to guide us, and, in time, to heal us.

Are you searching for new meaning as you navigate one of life's inevitable mid-course corrections? If so, you must place your faith, your trust, and your life in the hands of the One who does not change: your heavenly Father. He is the immovable rock upon which you must construct this day and every day. When you do, you are secure.

MORE FROM GOD'S WORD

Then He who sat on the throne said,
"Behold, I make all things new."
REVELATION 21:5 NKJV

I am the LORD, and I do not change.
MALACHI 3:6 NLT

When I was a child, I spoke like a child, I thought
like a child, I reasoned like a child. When I became
a man, I put aside childish things.
1 CORINTHIANS 13:11 HCSB

But grow in the grace and knowledge of our Lord
and Savior Jesus Christ. To Him be the glory both
now and forever. Amen.
2 PETER 3:18 NKJV

The wise see danger ahead and avoid it,
but fools keep going and get into trouble.
PROVERBS 22:3 NCV

MORE THOUGHTS ABOUT CHANGE

Sometimes your medicine bottle has on it, "Shake well before using." That is what God has to do with some of His people. He has to shake them well before they are ever usable.

VANCE HAVNER

Are you on the eve of change? Embrace it. Accept it. Don't resist it. Change is not only a part of life, change is a necessary part of God's strategy. To use us to change the world, He alters our assignments.

MAX LUCADO

There is no growth without change, no change without fear or loss, and no loss without pain.

RICK WARREN

Change always starts in your mind. The way you think determines the way you feel, and the way you feel influences the way you act.

RICK WARREN

The world changes—circumstances change, we change—but God's Word never changes.

WARREN WIERSBE

REMEMBER THIS

The world changes day by day and moment by moment. But God never changes. No matter what happens, you can always depend on Him.

GET PRACTICAL

Change is inevitable. Growth is not. God will come to your doorstep on countless occasions with opportunities to learn and to grow, and He will knock. Your challenge, of course, is to open the door.

A CONVERSATION STARTER

Talk to a friend about the inevitability of change and the trustworthiness of God.

NOTES TO YOURSELF
BIG CHANGES

Write down some of the important ways your world is changing and what you can do to adapt.

....

....

....

....

....

....

....

....

....

15

THE QUESTION

During tough times, I know that I need courage,
but sometimes courage is in short supply.
Where can I find it?

THE ANSWER

When tough times arrive (and they will), you
should guard your heart by turning it over to God.
Then work as if everything depended on you and
pray as if everything depended on Him.

*God is in control. He may not take away
trials or make detours for us, but He
strengthens us through them.*

BILLY GRAHAM

REDISCOVERING YOUR PURPOSE WHEN TIMES ARE TOUGH

We are hard-pressed on every side, yet not crushed; we are perplexed, but not in despair.

2 Corinthians 4:8 NKJV

Sometimes our blessings are easy to spot. When we accomplish our goals and our dreams come true, we find it easy to thank God and even easier to celebrate our victories. But what about the losses? How should we respond to God when our hopes are dashed and our dreams don't come true?

God has a plan for each of us, a plan that only He understands. That plan inevitably leads us over our fair share of mountaintops, but it also leads us through the darker valleys, the hard times we can't quite comprehend.

If you're experiencing tough times, don't despair, don't give in, and don't give up. Instead, consider the possibility that the trial you're enduring may be a way for God to reach you and teach you lessons you could learn no other way.

Perhaps your greatest disappointment is actually a blessing in disguise. Perhaps what you see as a stumbling block is actually God's stepping stone. Maybe your hard times are simply hard lessons, lessons that God in His infinite wisdom knows you need to learn.

MORE FROM GOD'S WORD

He heals the brokenhearted
and binds up their wounds.
Psalm 147:3 HCSB

The Lord is my shepherd; I shall not want.
Psalm 23:1 KJV

God blesses those who patiently endure testing
and temptation. Afterward they will
receive the crown of life that God has
promised to those who love him.
James 1:12 NLT

The Lord is my rock, my fortress, and my deliverer,
my God, my mountain where I seek refuge.
My shield, the horn of my salvation,
my stronghold, my refuge, and my Savior.
2 Samuel 22:2–3 HCSB

I called to the Lord in my distress; I called to
my God. From His temple He heard my voice.
2 Samuel 22:7 HCSB

MORE THOUGHTS
ABOUT ADVERSITY

*Human problems are never greater
than divine solutions.*

ERWIN LUTZER

*The truth is, God's strength is fully revealed
when our strength is depleted.*

LIZ CURTIS HIGGS

God alone can give us songs in the night.

C. H. SPURGEON

*Life is literally filled with God-appointed storms.
These squalls surge across everyone's horizon.
We all need them.*

CHARLES SWINDOLL

*Often God has to shut a door in our face
so that He can subsequently open the door
through which He wants us to go.*

CATHERINE MARSHALL

REMEMBER THIS

When we experience the inevitable disappointments and hardships of life, we do so with the ultimate armor: God's promises. When we ask for His guidance, He leads us along the right path: His path.

GET PRACTICAL

If your life has been turned upside down, you may find yourself searching for something new: a different direction, a new purpose, or a fresh start. As you make your plans, be sure to consult God. He never leaves you. Your task is to pray, to listen, and to follow His lead.

———⌇———

A CONVERSATION STARTER

Talk to a friend about ways that tough times help you grow spiritually and emotionally.

NOTES TO YOURSELF
OVERCOMING TOUGH TIMES

Write down your ideas about the best ways to find the courage and strength you'll need whenever you encounter tough times.

16

THE QUESTION

Sometimes it's hard to be an obedient Christian.
What does the Bible say about obedience?

THE ANSWER

God's Word is clear: obey Him or face the
consequences. The Lord rewards obedience and
punishes disobedience. So it's not enough to
understand His rules; you must also live by them.

*Let us never suppose that obedience is impossible
or that holiness is meant only for a select few.
Our Shepherd leads us in paths of righteousness—
not for our name's sake but for His.*

Elisabeth Elliot

TRUST AND OBEY

Trust in the Lord with all your heart, and lean not on your own understanding; in all your ways acknowledge Him, and He shall direct your paths.

PROVERBS 3:5–6 NKJV

God's instructions to mankind are contained in a book like no other: the Holy Bible. When we obey God's commandments and listen carefully to the conscience He has placed in our hearts, we are secure. But if we disobey our Creator, if we choose to ignore the teachings and the warnings of His Word, we do so at great peril.

If we believe in God, we should trust in God. Yet sometimes, when we are besieged by fears and doubts, trusting God is hard indeed. Trusting God means entrusting Him with every aspect of our lives as we follow His commandments and pray for His guidance. When we experience the inevitable pains of life here on earth, we must accept God's will and seek His healing touch. And at times we must be willing to wait patiently for God to reveal plans that only He can see.

So as you continue the search for purpose and meaning in this lifetime, what will you learn and whom will you trust? Will you take time to feed your mind and fill your heart? And will you study the guidebook that God has given you? Hopefully so, because His plans and His promises are waiting for you there, inside the covers of a book like no other: His Book. It contains the essential wisdom you'll need to navigate the seas of life and land safely on that distant shore.

MORE FROM GOD'S WORD

Those who trust in the LORD are like Mount Zion.
It cannot be shaken; it remains forever.
PSALM 125:1 HCSB

Jesus said, "Don't let your hearts be troubled.
Trust in God, and trust in me."
JOHN 14:1 NCV

Now by this we know that we know Him,
if we keep His commandments.
1 JOHN 2:3 NKJV

Praise the LORD! Happy are those who respect
the LORD, who want what he commands.
PSALM 112:1 NCV

Teach me, O LORD, the way of Your statutes,
and I shall observe it to the end.
PSALM 119:33 NASB

MORE THOUGHTS
ABOUT OBEDIENCE

*Faith and obedience are bound up in
the same bundle. He that obeys God, trusts God;
and he that trusts God, obeys God.*

C. H. SPURGEON

Obedience is the key to every door.

GEORGE MACDONALD

*Obedience is a foundational stepping-stone
on the path of God's will.*

ELIZABETH GEORGE

*Never be afraid to trust an unknown future
to a known God.*

CORRIE TEN BOOM

*Never imagine that you can be
a loser by trusting in God.*

C. H. SPURGEON

REMEMBER THIS

Because God is just, He rewards righteousness just as surely as He punishes sin. Obedience always earns God's pleasure; disobedience doesn't.

GET PRACTICAL

Obedience is one of the ways you can express your gratitude to God for the countless blessings He has given you.

—~—

A CONVERSATION STARTER

Talk to a friend about the rewards of obedience and the costs of disobedience.

NOTES TO YOURSELF
ABOUT OBEDIENCE

Write down a few thoughts about the rewards of obeying God's laws and the dangers of disobeying them.

17

THE QUESTION

I want to sense God's presence,
but it's not easy for me. What should I do?

THE ANSWER

First, remember that God isn't far away; He's right
here, right now; and He's ready to talk to you
right here, right now. So find a quiet place and
open your heart to Him. When you do, you'll sense
God's presence and His love, which, by the way,
is already surrounding you and your loved ones.

*For it is God who is working in you, enabling you
both to desire and to work out His good purpose.*

PHILIPPIANS 2:13 HCSB

YOU DON'T HAVE TO
DO IT ALONE

I am not alone, because the Father is with Me.
JOHN 16:32 NKJV

God is everywhere: everywhere you've ever been, everywhere you'll ever be. He is not absent from our world, nor is He absent from your world. God is not "out there"; He is "right here," continuously reshaping His universe, and continuously reshaping the lives of those who dwell in it.

Your Creator is with you always, listening to your thoughts and prayers, watching over your every move. If the demands of everyday life weigh down upon you, you may be tempted to ignore God's presence or—worse yet—to lose faith in His promises. But when you quiet yourself and acknowledge His presence, God will touch your heart and renew your strength.

Psalm 46:10 reminds us to "be still, and know that I am God" (NKJV). When we do, we can be comforted in the knowledge that God does not love us from a distance. He is not just near. He is here.

MORE FROM GOD'S WORD

Though I walk through the valley of the shadow of death, I will fear no evil: for thou art with me.

PSALM 23:4 KJV

For the eyes of Yahweh roam throughout the earth to show Himself strong for those whose hearts are completely His.

2 CHRONICLES 16:9 HCSB

I know the Lord is always with me. I will not be shaken, for he is right beside me.

PSALM 16:8 NLT

Draw near to God, and He will draw near to you.

JAMES 4:8 HCSB

Be still, and know that I am God.

PSALM 46:10 KJV

MORE THOUGHTS
ABOUT GOD'S PRESENCE

Do not limit the limitless God! With Him, face the future unafraid because you are never alone.

LETTIE COWMAN

Mark it down. You will never go where God is not.

MAX LUCADO

It is God to whom and with whom we travel;
while He is the end of our journey,
He is also at every stopping place.

ELISABETH ELLIOT

The Lord is the one who travels every mile of
the wilderness way as our leader, cheering us,
supporting and supplying and fortifying us.

ELISABETH ELLIOT

God is an infinite circle
whose center is everywhere.

ST. AUGUSTINE

REMEMBER THIS

God isn't far away—He's right here, right now. And He's willing to talk to you right here, right now.

GET PRACTICAL

Having trouble hearing God? If so, slow yourself down, tune out the distractions, and listen carefully. God has important things to say; your task is to be still and to listen.

—⁓—

A CONVERSATION STARTER

Talk to a friend about what it feels like to sense God's presence in the midst of everyday life.

NOTES TO YOURSELF
SENSING GOD'S PRESENCE

Write down your favorite places to read the Bible, to pray, and to contemplate God's plans for your life.

....

....

....

....

....

....

....

....

....

....

....

18

THE QUESTION

Sometimes I'm so impatient. What does the Bible say about trusting God's timing?

THE ANSWER

The Bible makes it clear that God's timing is best, so don't allow yourself to become discouraged if things don't work out as quickly as you wish. Instead of worrying about your future, entrust it to God. He knows exactly what you need and exactly when you need it.

We often hear about waiting on God, which actually means that He is waiting until we are ready. There is another side, however. When we wait for God, we are waiting until He is ready.

LETTIE COWMAN

TRUST HIS TIMING

He has made everything appropriate in its time.
He has also put eternity in their hearts,
but man cannot discover the work
God has done from beginning to end.

ECCLESIASTES 3:11 HCSB

Perhaps you're anxious to begin the next phase of your life's journey. If you're like most people, you're in a hurry. You know precisely what you want, and you know precisely when you want it: as soon as possible. Because your time on earth is limited, you may feel a sense of urgency. God does not. There is no panic in heaven.

Our heavenly Father, in His infinite wisdom, operates according to His own timetable, not ours. He has plans that we cannot see and purposes that we cannot know. He has created a world that unfolds according to His own schedule. Thank goodness! After all, He is omniscient; His is trustworthy; and He knows what's best for us.

If you've been waiting impatiently for the Lord to answer your prayers, it's time to put a stop to all that needless worry. You can be sure that God will answer your prayers when the time is right. You job is to keep praying—and working—until He does.

MORE FROM GOD'S WORD

Therefore humble yourselves under the mighty hand of God, that He may exalt you in due time.

1 Peter 5:6 NKJV

Those who trust in the Lord are like Mount Zion. It cannot be shaken; it remains forever.

Psalm 125:1 HCSB

Yet the Lord longs to be gracious to you; therefore he will rise up to show you compassion. For the Lord is a God of justice. Blessed are all who wait for him!

Isaiah 30:18 NIV

Trust in the Lord with all your heart, and lean not on your own understanding; in all your ways acknowledge Him, and He shall direct your paths.

Proverbs 3:5–6 NKJV

To every thing there is a season, and a time to every purpose under the heaven.

Ecclesiastes 3:1 KJV

MORE THOUGHTS
ABOUT GOD'S TIMING

*Teach us, O Lord, the disciplines of patience,
for to wait is often harder than to work.*

PETER MARSHALL

*The Christian's journey through life
isn't a sprint but a marathon.*

BILLY GRAHAM

*Waiting on God brings us to the journey's end
quicker than our feet.*

LETTIE COWMAN

*We often hear about waiting on God, which
actually means that He is waiting until we are
ready. There is another side, however. When we
wait for God, we are waiting until He is ready.*

LETTIE COWMAN

*We must learn to move according to the timetable
of the Timeless One, and to be at peace.*

ELISABETH ELLIOT

REMEMBER THIS

God is never early or late. He's always on time. Although you don't know precisely what you need—or when you need it—He does. So trust His timing.

GET PRACTICAL

Perhaps you're in a hurry to understand God's unfolding plan for your life. If so, remember that He operates according to a perfect timetable. That timetable is His, not yours. So be patient.

—∿∿—

A CONVERSATION STARTER

Talk to a friend about what it means to wait patiently for God.

NOTES TO YOURSELF
TRUSTING GOD'S TIMING

Write down your thoughts about the rewards of patience and perseverance.

19

THE QUESTION

What does the Bible say about discipleship?

THE ANSWER

God's Word makes it clear: we are all called to
follow in Christ's footsteps. So, when it comes to
discipleship, you owe it to yourself, to your family,
and to your Creator be a devoted follower
of the One from Galilee.

—⁂—

A disciple is a follower of Christ.
That means you take on His priorities as your own.
His agenda becomes your agenda.
His mission becomes your mission.

CHARLES STANLEY

YOU ARE A DISCIPLE

"Follow Me," Jesus told them, "and I will make you fish for people!" Immediately they left their nets and followed Him.

MARK 1:17-18 HCSB

Jesus instructed His disciples that each one must take up his cross daily and follow Him. The disciples must have known exactly what the Christ meant. In Jesus's day, prisoners were forced to carry their own crosses to the place where they would be put to death. Thus, Christ's message was clear: in order to follow Him, the disciples must deny themselves and, instead, trust Him completely. Nothing has changed since then.

If we are to be disciples of God's Son, we must trust Him and place Him at the very center of our lives. Jesus never comes "next." He is always first. The paradox, of course, is that only by sacrificing ourselves to Him do we gain salvation for ourselves.

Do you want to be a real follower of the One from Galilee? Then pick up His cross today and every day. When you do, He'll bless you now and forever.

MORE FROM GOD'S WORD

For whoever wants to save his life will lose it,
but whoever loses his life because of Me
and the gospel will save it.

MARK 8:35 HCSB

How happy is everyone who fears the LORD,
who walks in His ways!

PSALM 128:1 HCSB

Follow God's example, therefore,
as dearly loved children.

EPHESIANS 5:1 NIV

Then Jesus spoke to them again: "I am the light
of the world. Anyone who follows Me will never
walk in the darkness but will have the light of life."

JOHN 8:12 HCSB

Whoever wants to be my disciple must deny
themselves and take up their cross and follow me.

MARK 8:34 NIV

MORE THOUGHTS
ABOUT DISCIPLESHIP

*Jesus challenges you and me to
keep our focus daily on the cross of His will
if we want to be His disciples.*

ANNE GRAHAM LOTZ

*Discipleship usually brings us into the necessity
of choice between duty and desire.*

ELISABETH ELLIOT

*His voice leads us not into timid discipleship
but into bold witness.*

CHARLES STANLEY

*To be a disciple of Jesus means to learn from Him,
to follow Him. The cost may be high.*

BILLY GRAHAM

*Our Lord's conception of discipleship is not that we
work for God, but that God works through us.*

OSWALD CHAMBERS

REMEMBER THIS

Jesus has invited you to become His disciple. If you accept His invitation—if you follow Him and obey His commandments—you will be protected and blessed.

GET PRACTICAL

Today, think of at least one step you can take to become a better disciple for Christ. Then, take that step.

—⁓—

A CONVERSATION STARTER

Talk to a friend about specific ways you can follow more closely in Christ's footsteps.

NOTES TO YOURSELF
ABOUT DISCIPLESHIP

Write down your thoughts about what it means to be a true disciple of Jesus.

....

....

....

....

....

....

....

....

....

20

THE QUESTION

Sometimes it's easy for me to lose perspective.
When it happens, what should I do?

THE ANSWER

When we lose perspective, God's Word
teaches us to slow down, to calm down,
and to pray. When you ask God to
restore your perspective, He will do it.

To know the will of God is the highest of all wisdom.

BILLY GRAHAM

PERSPECTIVE AND PEACE

*Joyful is the person who finds wisdom,
the one who gains understanding.*

PROVERBS 3:13 NLT

Life in the twenty-first century can be busy and complicated. Amid the rush and crush of the daily grind, it's easy to lose perspective, it's easy to become frustrated, and it's easy to lose sight of the real reason God put us here.

When our world seems to be spinning out of control, we can regain perspective by slowing ourselves down and then turning our thoughts and prayers toward the Creator of the universe. When we do, He calms our spirits and restores our sense of perspective.

Do you carve out quiet moments each day to praise your Creator? You should. The familiar words of Psalm 46:10 remind us to "be still, and know that I am God" (NKJV). When we do, we encounter the awesome presence of our loving heavenly Father, and we are blessed beyond words. But if we ignore the presence of our Creator, we rob ourselves of His perspective, His peace, and His joy.

Today and every day, make time to be still before God. When you do, you can face the day's complications with the wisdom and power that only He can provide.

MORE FROM GOD'S WORD

If you teach the wise, they will get knowledge.
Proverbs 21:11 NCV

The one who acquires good sense loves himself;
one who safeguards understanding finds success.
Proverbs 19:8 HCSB

Since you have been raised to new life with Christ,
set your sights on the realities of heaven, where
Christ sits in the place of honor at God's right hand.
Colossians 3:1 NLT

Teach me, Lord, the meaning of Your statutes,
and I will always keep them.
Psalm 119:33 HCSB

Trust in the Lord with all your heart
and lean not on your own understanding.
Proverbs 3:5 NIV

MORE THOUGHTS ABOUT PERSPECTIVE

When you are experiencing the challenges of life, perspective is everything.

JONI EARECKSON TADA

Joy is the direct result of having God's perspective on our daily lives and the effect of loving our Lord enough to obey His commands and trust His promises.

BILL BRIGHT

God's peace and perspective are available to you through His Word.

ELIZABETH GEORGE

The world appears very little to a soul that contemplates the greatness of God.

BROTHER LAWRENCE

REMEMBER THIS

When you focus on the world, you lose perspective. When you focus on God's promises and His love, you gain clearer perspective. Keep your focus on God and His plans for your life.

GET PRACTICAL

Your life is an integral part of God's grand plan. So don't become unduly upset over the minor inconveniences of life, and don't worry too much about today's setbacks—they're temporary.

A CONVERSATION STARTER

Talk to a friend about perspective: how you lose it and how you regain it.

NOTES TO YOURSELF
MAINTAINING PERSPECTIVE

Write down your thoughts about the need to maintain a proper perspective about life on earth and eternal life in heaven.